Seance

Jacob Moses

This book is dedicated to my familiars

Author's Note (House-Tree-Person)

The House-Tree-Person Assessment (HTP) is used for the diagnosis of mental functioning and personality issues. Although art therapists generally do not administer this test, it is incorporated into psychological examinations. Employers often use the HTP to examine the psyche of potential employees. When I was pursuing a certificate in Creative Arts Therapy at The New School, I took this test and will examine my process of how the images came into fruition.

I was assigned to draw a house, a tree, and a person on separate sheets of paper in pencil. The next step was to draw a house, a tree, and a person on separate sheets of paper in crayon. The images did not need to be the same. Afterwards, I was directed to write some notes after I finished. Overall, I did see patterns in my drawings. The following author's note will demonstrate these patterns, as well as the mood shift that transpired as I was drawing.

~~~~~~

House (pencil)

The first house that came to mind was a four family brick house in Staten Island, NY. I lived there from 1983 to 1996. Most of my youth, from age two to age fifteen, was spent with my mother and father, as well as three other families. I remember the names of the kids like it was yesterday. Their names were Nadine, Mitchell, Milena, Jesse, Alex, and Laura. Our families were very close knit. Many summers would be spent sitting on our porch, lighting firecrackers on July 4th, and catching fireflies. Before a new landlord controlled the building, there was a chain-linked gate and rosebushes that ensured our privacy from the rest of the neighborhood. Afterwards, the bushes were chopped down
~~~~~~

and the bricks were covered in concrete. Throughout my youth, it was as if we lived in a castle. These were carefree times. I immediately knew this would be my first image, as it brought me the most joy while waxing nostalgic.

Tree (pencil)

The first tree I envisioned was my Chanukah bush. While many of my Christian neighbors were trimming their Christmas trees, we trimmed a Chanukah bush. Although the origin of the tree escapes my memory, it was an integral part of my youth during the winter season. The tree was adorned with an eclectic array of ornaments and blinking lights. I used very little effort in depicting this tree, as my exact recollection of it is uncertain. My parents and I attempted to recreate the Chanukah tradition in our current residence. The feeling was far from the same. The bush was as much a part of my neighbor's tradition as it was mine.

Person (pencil)

I instinctively knew the first person I would draw was my father. He passed away on June 11th, 2013. This was six days before my birthday and a week after I began my certificate program at The New School. Everybody who knew my father were immediately drawn to him. They especially fell in love with his accent, as he was born in Johannesburg, South Africa. He had a stroke at the age of twenty, leaving the right side of his body paralyzed. Although the stroke was a challenge, he persevered through it by cognitively retraining himself to speak, walk, and write. He met my mother in Israel. They got married about two years after meeting and remained together for over forty years. He especially beat the odds by finding a job as a research chemist at Hoffmann-La Roche. His cause of death was another stroke, which affected the left side of his body. I witnessed it occur, not knowing that this would be the last day my dad would spend in his home. As I type this, I am still very much in mourning. It still seems too soon.

House (crayon)

The second house is a stylized version of my current residence in Staten Island, NY. While my condo is actually white and brown, the colors I used were black and gray, as I find living there to be dismal. I do not have the same happiness here that I did in my previous residence. In fact, I find that I have more bad memories than good in this house and consider the neighborhood to be a mecca of conformity. Mental health issues arose during my adolescence. Episodes occurred within a span of the first seven years of living here. Since the houses are attached, I can often hear my neighbors screaming and witness them gossiping about other people in the development. I usually try to fly under the radar. I made the sky different shades of blue, as the sky is always bluer outside of the development. I often seek refuge in places that are natural, such as Willowbrook Park. This segues into my next image.

Tree (crayon)

This tree represents my desperate need for sanctuary. I always visit one particular tree in Willowbrook Park, located across the street from the development. I have taken numerous pictures of it through the years. Every season is represented in my collection of digital photos. The photos do more justice to the tree than the picture I drew from memory. Oftentimes, I have used this tree for shade and to write poetry underneath the branches. The park itself brings me delight, especially the wide variety of waterfowl. I have seen ducks, geese, swans, and cranes swim through Willowbrook Pond. I often walked around that pond for exercise. I often listened to my iPod and played Pink

Floyd's *The Dark Side of the Moon* as I was walking. The music and nature always made for a good walk through the park.

Person (crayon)

The stick figure with the burning head and question marks is me. By the time I got to this drawing, I had become exhausted. However, I think this drawing was the most conceptual out of the six. Naturally, it represents confusion and frustration. I specifically picked the colors of the question marks to represent halftone printing colors (cyan, magenta, yellow, and black). I studied graphic design in college and eventually I was overwhelmed by the field and was unsure whether I wanted to pursue it as a career. I set my head on fire because of the constant flotsam and jetsam of my thoughts and the hyperactive energy that currently exists in my mind. Given that green is my favorite color, I made the stick figure green. Oftentimes, I am still confused and need to give myself some direction in life. It bececame burdensome to organize my thoughts, especially when it felt like they are racing like cars in the Indianapolis 500.

~~~~~~

Throughout this process, I noticed a trend. With the pencil drawings, I was able to reflect on pleasant memories; with the crayon drawings, I started to sink deep into depression. Perhaps the reason behind this lies in the supplies. Oftentimes, the pencil represents more control and the crayon represents less control. The pencil images were more relaxed, as the pencil point was more relaxed when I drew. In fact, it glided in my hand. The crayons were more burdensome, as I was pressing hard on the paper and felt a sense of anxiety and even rage as I was drawing with them.
~~~~~~

Another thing worth mentioning was the regression I felt as I was drawing. One regression took place with the pencil drawings. These were the good times in my past that were represented. I was much happier in the past. The crayon drawings represented a regression to adverse feelings rising to the surface. It represented the sadness in my life and the aftermath of how I felt after my father passed away.

Overall, these drawings were a tell-tale sign that I needed a certain level of peace that I used to feel when I was much younger. I went into this assignment thinking that the color would be more of a liberating aspect to these drawings. In reality, the opposite occurred. I regressed to places I least expected to go. Before this assessment was administered, I had an idea as to what I would draw. However, the feelings that would be evoked were a mystery.

In conclusion, this was an interesting assignment. Certain feelings I have repressed over the years came to the surface as I was drawing. Every time I did an experiential in this class, I discovered a part of myself that I never knew existed. This is the reason I would like to incorporate art therapy into a private practice. Sometimes, the art is the only salvation for one who suffers and is a form of expression more effective than spoken words. The images I drew represented more of my true emotions. At the very moment that this test was administered, words would have been inadequate to purge my inner demons.

13 Iyar 5780

"You fondle my trigger, then you blame my gun."

-Fiona Apple

Contents

Seance

se·ance

/ˈsāˌäns/

noun

a meeting at which people attempt to make contact with the dead, especially through the agency of a medium.

Genesis of Jacob

(Published in Auroras & Blossoms)

On the pink moon, I left behind a dozen years of instability
A tribe was born for every year I tossed insanity into the forge
Each tribe presented a gift rising from these sacrifices
My darkness illuminated by the rising sun of Reuben
My walls excavated through subterfuge of Simeon
My heart protected through vision of Levi
My weakness absolved via the lion's heart of Judah
My justice calibrated through the scales of Dan
My kindness liberated by the doe of Naphtali
My community connected with the tents of Gad
My peace harvested within the olives of Asher
My universe explored through observations of Issachar
My finances supplemented by the travels of Zebulon
My dreams realized through many prophecies of Joseph
My sacrifices rationed through the appetite of Benjamin
Indiscretions   Sacrileges   Lamentations   Transgressions
I become the Genesis in which my evolution tells me that
Jacob is who I must be
I await the Exodus in which my revolution tells me
that Israel is who I must embody
I am the healing force who dwells in gardens
inherently nourished
I am the poet who has survived long enough
to scribe his legacy

Willow in the Wind
(Published in Dreams Walking)

```
     ^^^^^^^^^^^^^^^^^^^^^^^^^^^^^^^^^^^^^^^^^^^^^^^^^^
    ^^^^^^^^^^^^^^^^^^^^^^^^^^^^^^^^^^^^^^^^^^^^^^^^^^^^^^
   ^^^^^^^^^^^^^^^^^^^^^^^^^^^^^^^^^^^^^^^^^^^^^^^^^^^^^^^^^^
  ^^^^^^^^^^^^^^^^^^^^^^^^^^^^^^^^^^^^^^^^^^^^^^^^^^^^^^^^^^^^^

^^^^^^  *****  Wind comforts      my soul      and as sure as   *****      ^^^^^^
I am the      ****** @@          weeping tree  @@    ******           which will simply
  ******  Laugh with  _____        \        /  ______        the breezes  ******
   Lay in the soil  ***   -----    |        | -----  ***  my branches will not
   Only sway near the grass _____\        /_______________but I always
   Wave without the      -----    \      /  -----  threat of a clean break
              @@@@@@       \      /   @@@@@@
```

Forgiveness

So many times, I have just walked away
Occasionally, I have forgiven
Sometimes, I take my anger day by day
Don't want to disappear for a living
My magic is meant to craft divine charms
I rarely use abilities to hex
Will not initiate magic that harms
Unless your intent is simply to vex
Virtue of patience and forgiveness last
So long as reconciliation reigns
Too hungry for companionship to fast
Too hurt for more excruciating pains
I need to place forgiveness in my heart
I need to forgive myself for my part

Parakeet Song

All shall hail King Darius in a white cage
Never saw the creation of a palace
Lived inside a bachelor pad of a birdcage
Blue and white martyr

O' Queen Jane, albino, white feathers, red eyes
She most likely overthrowing King Darius
On one summer day, he wound up flat lining
She was the culprit

Kofi - green and yellow bird was the next one
Womanizer, fought with Queen Jane immensely
Met a bad demise as one of four budgies
Must have been hen pecked

We must never forget about King Saffron
Father of three chicks and he is still reigning
Yellow feathers, green and black accents, boldness
Dedicated dad

Frost - the matriarch of the tallest mansion
Lost one chick, she laid five more eggs, maternal
Three hatched, lovely indigo feathers, soulful
Death by egg binding

Green-yellow, Safari was once a free range
Took up residence in my mother's chamber
Lost Queen Jane, loved her with undying passion
Local adventures

Amazon - the white bird donned in confetti
Keeps to himself - chronically transcendental
Roommate with Safari - it seems to have worked
Now they are buddies

Koa - first born, yellow with wingtips blackened
Pride of Frost and King Saffron, birthright offered
Sits on swings and rocks, overlooking the sun
Heart of Hawaii

Epic now is Erica, yellow also
Speckled with gray feathers, poised like a leopard
Now Safari's main squeeze, he dances for her
Eyes of affection

Last born Sigil - Frost and King Saffron's baby
Faintly silver accents adorn bright yellow
Quiet - but observant from every view of
Her tail's flirtations

Colecovision

Our cursors will keep all our ghosts at bay
Eat strife like burgers we prepare to build
Fight cosmic gangsters standing in the way
Lift fallen soldiers over war-torn hills
Driving though harsh conditions dodging guns
Aiming for flying ducks diving through screens
Pinball soaring through seas under the sun
Our futures set our psychedelic scenes
These unicycle wheels must learn to leap
Hopping upon these color changing cubes
Solar system conquest: blip, bloop, and bleep
Root beer shall flow from inside fountain tubes
Two quarters in the slot will buy your games
It's not over until you type your name

Golden's Deli

Kosher style deli
Ordered pastrami on rye
French fries on the side
Pareve egg cream satiates
While sitting on the A train
Subway car intact
Settled in the dining hall
Where I sit and nosh
To my youthful heart's content
May its memory live on

Lingua Franca

(Published in Verse-Virtual)

Love languages, eclectic at their core
But they coincide with the universe
Our tongues operate the same more and more
Through crises, we too embrace the diverse
While we spend all our quarantine alone
This common ground we share will emanate
Decoding of the philosopher's stone
Reveals the dialect of human faith
Whether English or Spanish or Russian
Whether Chinese or Arabic or French
A poet's words will not cease in touching
Will not keep us trapped in this solemn trench
COVID-19 preys on the strong and weak
In turn, it's given us the words to speak

The Revolution

(Published in Verse-Virtual)

We will be the survivors of this:
Planning how to weather the storms of Armageddon

Tools at our disposal fueled by space:
That which we provide and the cosmos where we orbit

No longer do we need to assault:
In reality, our uprising is one of healing

We are already in agitation:
Protection in our hands; we are the gifts provided

In the midst of divine vision quests:
Shamanic ties between us and ancestral guidance

Periods become semicolons:
Stories still need to be told, for we are still at war

Now I find myself in this battle:
One which puts me on the front lines of viral ambush

I've got my altar to protect me:
Grapes and honey, Dionysus and Lakshmi appeased

Enriched by herbal sacraments of marijuana:
She will calm my anxiety and my depression

Masks I've worn no longer protect me:
They were the kind hiding all of my identities

My words have never been sanitized:
Though now the hands with which I write them are doused in Purell

But I'm not afraid to get dirty:
Paint and ink still are my weapons while we're struggling

Revolution is upon us now:
The kind where artists have enough time for creation

One Year Sober

Mastery of light
shone upon the body of
a healing soldier

Pretenses, façades
which no longer serve to mask
spiritual death

Now a corpse lies still
Passersby no longer see
his possessed body

In the heavens, he
will learn how to be in touch
with his emotions

He will keep moving
as he yearns to right the wrongs
upon this planet

In his alchemy
transformative journeys will
detoxify him

He will pass the gates
which lead to a heaven
unseen on this earth

Love will greet him there

He will know the meaning of
sharing affection

Bountiful chest of
gold transmuted through the task
of self-reflection

He will greet the world
resurrected by promise
of a clearer path

His gifts will bestow
Trees from seeds buried within
a once barren land
Now he comes back down
after stars guide him through his
resuscitation

Vision now restored
consciousness acute, now he
is alive again

Isolation

I am alone
scared of my shadow
peering through the cracks
of a dimly lit office

Scared of my shadow
filling each corner
of a dimly lit office
which sits in the basement

Filling each corner
in my brain is a demon
which sits in the basement
succumbing to heat

In my brain is a demon
working effortlessly while I am
succumbing to heat
trapped inside these walls

Working effortlessly while I am
peering through these cracks
trapped inside these walls
I am alone

Essential

(Published in Verse-Virtual)

Every time I wake from
Slumber, I am more easily
Startled during morning, noon, and
Evening hours; terror purveyed by
Networks and cables and satellites
Televising this necessary foray into
Introversion; which I no longer
Attribute to shyness, but the
Loneliness thrust upon the masses

This Isn't Happening

I am trying to get though this morass
These endless days of boredom will pervade
My patience dying with melancholy
Alacrity I attempt to maintain
All the while wishing this was all a dream
Overtly dreaming and screaming aloud

This isn't happening

Especially maintaining sanity
I'm shuffling in this psychotic mess
Some still consider me the enemy
Dissenting against this autocracy
Plutocracy and oligarchy reign
Consumed by blatant demagoguery
Controlled by a megalomaniac
Wishing by some miracle of Hashem

This isn't happening

But now I'm staying somewhat productive
Attempting to write though all my anguish
Passing through life as phantoms of sickness
It's been too long since I've seen the ocean
Compassion agitated through his mess
My empathy will survive so long as

This isn't happening

Land of the Night

Multitude of earth
dwelling nocturnal
creatures, blissful

in the links between
shadows and ecstasy
Into this moon, stare

deep into the heaven
in between clouds, on
top of quasars, burst

of the nebulous, rain
distantly reflects
desires of id, libido

quenched by red wine
Dance of midnight, an
aphorism, primal ego
,
unpredictable yaw, a
shift of levity, moor
where roses fly east

Retrograde orbit, we
will undo these wars
Reneged prophecies

Apocalyptic refund
Golden ratio intact
Aesthetically pure

is this celebration
Collective indigo
intuits connection

Missing Cup

In the beginning
we learn to spell

Upon my altar
were four aces
from my tarot deck

Aces are elements
in their purest form

Medium of the spirit
directed by symbiosis

Come the witching hour
wands still commanded fire
air surrounded the sword
treasures of pentacles buried in the earth

But the water in this cup
evaporated into the atmosphere

Perhaps a reminder
that my altar
was overabundant with emotion

That my invocations
accepted my heart
as an ultimate offering

As honey jars
sealed my fortune

As thirteen pennies
supplemented the soil

As nails in a jar of urine
protected my yard

As the carcasses of mice
inside a clay planter
gave birth to
Purple Deadnettle

St. Michael watches over me
Violet rays hazy and ultra sage

Qualities which prove
pills are not needed
to witness
majesties in mountains

Grapes to Dionysus
must have fermented
in this cup

Lakshmi must have
lined it with gold

In the end
we become magick

Survivor

(Published in Unspoken Word)

Twenty years
of the show Survivor
never prepared us for pandemics

Our fire
must always keep roaring
as we aim not to be extinguished

We're the tribe
of castaways who dare
to dream amid COVID-19 panic

Aligned are
stars and fraternity
even within lonely domiciles

The tag line:
Outwit, Outplay, Outlast
is appropriate for our struggles

Villainous
is this contagion
to which we need an immunity

The chorus
of these ancient voices
echo sentiments of starvation

Please tell me
if the tribe has spoken
to the souls of those unfit to breathe

Is it worth
one million fucking bucks
to stay stuck on this infected land?

We are not
playing a game right now
as we attempt to maintain our lives

No TV
can alleviate the
harsh terrains of our reality

Unscripted
casualties of disease
won't nullify our democracy

And now here
we are on this landscape
fearing every single element

Fishing for
a cure for all our ills
off the shore of our dystopia

Maintaining
our standing in this world
as we play this antisocial game

Torches are
standing tall as we walk
through these harsh terrains of maladies

Survivor:
forty seasons of grit
never prepared castaways for this

When You Can't Dream

(Published by NYPL: St. George Library)

Last night
all my dreams
were jumbled

Woke up
in a state
of confusion

Slept again
and still...
I was unaware
of the content
of these fuzzy
remnants of vision

Could it be
a manifestation
of bipolar
mixed states?

Maybe yet
another
situation
where my
mind was
too fragile
to see clearly

I am not
engaging
well with
lack of
stimulation

Too much distance
between me and
my light

Too little space
between me and
my shadows

Imaginings
pervaded by
deficiency
of clarity

Sickness
and the fear
of fever
manifests
sadness
and paranoia

No longer
chalked up
to one
mental
health
diagnosis

To be bipolar
in a scattered world
is to be a compass

Demagnetized
and without
a clear direction
out of melancholy

Amethyst Camel

Amethyst camel
Crested in the finest gold
Leads the caravan
Mother's spirit animal
Infused with father's birthstone

Chimney

I
Am
Red
Tall
Brick
Layers
Chimney
Standing
Exhausted
Monolithic
Resurrected
Renaissances

Other books by Jacob Moses

...and the willow smiled
http://cyberwit.net/publications/1245

Art Therapy 101
http://cyberwit.net/publications/1289

Special Thanks

Douglas G. Cala
Morningstar
Wil Wynn
Dr. Marguerite Maria Rivas
Commander
Sri
Mama Dukes
Papa Reggie
The Professor
Orion
Dumpling
Citrona
Double E
Gypsy Goat Child
Quess The Scholar
Ashman
Petey Red

...and all of our poetic ancestors for keeping this craft alive...
...Jacob Moses, Wizard of Willow, signing off...

שלום

Peace

Reviews of *Seance* (The Coven)

"Seance is the perfect balance of sadness, nostalgia, and sur-vival; hooking you right from the outset with the author's note (its bittersweet brilliance effectively framing the central themes of the book) and maintaining that magnetism til the very end. A few of my favorite pieces being: Land of the Night, Golden's Deli, Willow in the Wind, and Colecovision, which hearkens to the nostalgia element mentioned earlier (the rise and fall of arcade culture and the wane of innocence). Overall, Seance is a much-needed introspection for our isolation addled minds."

-Jared Rich, co-author of *Offerings*

"Jacob reaches deep into the diverse wells of his identity and brings up for his readers sustenance – wonderment – despair — and hope, survival elements for the journey he imagines for us. From the Twelve Tribes of Israel, through animals, dreams, angels, and Covid-19 escape/immersion, we share in the "...col-lective indigo..." that characterizes this time. Yes, this is hap-pening. Yes, he makes it happen."

-Margaret Chase, poet/performer/playwright

"The realms of the occult, mental health, and Judaism in Jacob Moses' poetry. His words breathe life and insight into readers' minds, especially during a time of uncertainty, fear, and quarantine. This book is further proof that the intertwined spirits of poetry and magic are alive and well in his writings."

-Ghia Vitale, senior editor of *Quail Bell Magazine*

"In ways both playful and ponderous, Seance evokes that inner numinous well which we all need in these weighty times."

-Ben Sumrall, theatre/media artist

"With his incredible work, Seance, author Jacob Moses takes you on a journey within that all who are spiritually minded can empathize with. It is a common misconception that the spiritual realm is a realm different from our, but the reality is that our realm is merely an expression of the spiritual. Through his insights into issues that plague us all, as well as his examinations of the occurrences of everyday life, Mr. Moses embodies the living art of poetry and self expression through the proverbial quill and ink. Give this book a read, you will thank yourself for doing so and you will find yourself feeling so much less alone in a world ravaged by COVID-19 and quarantine."

-Andrew Littlefield, poet/recovery advocate

"Seance by Jacob Moses, becomes a voice from Staten Island to the rest of the city, the clear call of poetry in the darkness of its quiet streets, imprisoned souls that do not mean harm but are full of wisdom and the poetic tone that whispers the genuine words of survival to COVID-19, the pandemic that has our city inside the walls, awaiting for freedom like the birds on Parakeet Song. The poet declares, "I am the healing force who dwells in gardens..." (Genesis of Jacob). When I started reading the book, another poet came to my mind, Guillaume Apollinaire, the passionate and prolific writer that coined the words "cubism" and "surrealism". He is also known for the calligrams, aesthetic poetry reunited in figures, visual art that combines form and function. Seance uses calligrams as a way to initiate us in the liturgy of a poetic order that absorbs religions, races, back-

grounds, and more. Willow in the Wind is a good example. I would like to point to the perfection of Chimney, whose choice of words achieve the essence of the book."

-Rocío Uchofen, author of *Geometría de la Urbe*

"Jacob Moses' Seance is an unusual and intelligent tour-de-force of the author's struggle for and with identity. The book is complex: in the Author's Note, we are given a rich background of psychological experience from which the poems later emerge as manifestations, embodiments of the author's quest for self-understanding. The poems themselves are explorations and answers to the underlying question, "What am I." The variety of the poems' styles help us identify how experience sculpts the Self, even as we struggle with our own challenging circumstances. Mr. Moses has gone to great lengths to express his search for meaning and is to be commended for the discipline inherent in his craft. With this book, he successfully summons the Muse and, in so doing, allows us to search for the Miraculous inherent in our own lives."

-Wil Wynn, author /publisher

"Jacob Moses has birthed a timely book with poems that proceed with a push, urgent rising as if through a burning ambush. Although presumably written alone, the poems communicate to all of us in isolation and unite with words waiting to touch. He is more than a medium, he's a Double XL talent who tarot deals a wheel of royal flushes that leaves parting red C's for A pluses. Moses' poems unlatch the imagination with their unique forms, reflect personally on love, loss and longing, and will make you crave a hug almost as much as a pastrami on rye. So say aah for Seance with an open mind, open heart and open mouth."

-Scottt Raven, author of *Sconnettts*/co-founder of Mayhem Poets.

"Everyone has a story to tell, but poets have a unique way of telling their story which gives a feast for the senses. You'll find your eyes jumping back and forth across the delicate papers following the adventures within his mind. Personal favorites include Parakeet Song, Isolation, and Willow in the Wind."

-Carissa Pignatelli, author of *Center Peace*

"After reading through Jacob Moses' Seance, I am reminded of why writers write. I am reminded of why readers read. I am reminded of this paradoxical idea that often characterizes the human condition and experience. This being that we often feel very much alone, and by telling our stories we can do a better job understanding ourselves and each other as we begin to make sense of a very difficult journey toward growth. Seance brings the reader on a journey through the past, the present, and is a fine example about how doing so can be frightening, but so impactful and necessary. Golden's Deli sent me on a stroll down memory lane that was much needed in these times."

-Zach Katz, MHC-LP, MSED

"I loved the author's note. It gave a really cool glimpse into him and his journey, but not in a typical, boring way. I don't even usually read that section in books, but he got me to read his. Overall, it feels like a journey of self-exploration and healing that gets jolted by the pandemic and then swept with the wave. I thought Genesis of Jacob was a dope way to start out. It really encompasses the work very well. Willow in the Wind, Forgiveness, Lingua Franca, Land of the Night, Missing Cup and When You Can't Dream were the ones that struck me the deepest. It's like a call to continued action and a solid pillar to lean on when you need to regroup."

-Thoughtress, performance poet

"While prior collections of the authors' poetry focused on battling, and grappling with his demons, Seance sees Jacob as an artist liberated and more in-control of himself. He accomplishes this adroitly and nimbly by peeling back layers and unlocking aspects of himself that were previously shut. Many of the pieces are refreshing with a matured voice and clear, accessible tones and themes. By this point in Jacob's career as a poet - both written and performative - the author truly exorcises his hurdles and the result is life-affirming and filled with comfort. By the end of Seance the reader gets the feeling that Jacob has reached new plateaus within himself and his craft. And, while he still may struggle, his confident grasp of language and self-understanding provides notable and worthwhile insights into an evolved artist."

-Douglas G. Cala, media/IT professional/social critic/performance poet

Richard Fragiacomo

(1943-2020)

श्राद्ध - 7"7 - Àṣẹ

Darren Darren

(1969-2020)